MY MATCH

MY MATCH

A satirical look at my
online dating adventures

Darren James

To order additional copies of this book, contact:
Xlibris Corporation
1-888-795-4274
www.Xlibris.com
Orders@Xlibris.com
46876

CONTENTS

DEDICATION

Over the past few years, I have met hundreds, yes hundreds, of terrific women through online dating. Many of them I am proud to call my friends. Perhaps they weren't "the one," but these relationships have taught me a lot; helped me learn about myself and my life, and I am a better man for it. For that I am grateful.

I dedicate this book to all of them. After all, it's the least I could do.

INTRODUCTION

Training Wheels

I never set out to write a book, at least not one about my online dating escapades. As a divorced guy over 40 and having been married for twenty years, I had simply intended to use the Internet as a way to get my feet wet, and get back into the dating scene, and to learn how to date all over again. *Training wheels*, if you will.

Tired of the club and bar scene (like many people, men and women, out there), I simply wanted to give online dating a try. I had no illusions of utopia, but thought that I could meet some new girlfriends and perhaps find another mate. So, I did some research on the dating websites that are out there and I had at it. I'm the kind of guy that always seems to learn things the hard way, and I didn't know how overwhelming it could be.

Unfortunately, with a personality like mine, you never do things in moderation. I became obsessed with, or rather addicted to, online dating. It consumed much of my time, days and nights. I spent a considerable amount of time doing searches on the dating websites, reading profiles, sending out email messages and answering responses.

My dating became an elaborate process and I was very methodical, printing out profiles and keeping extensive records on the many telephone conversations and dates with the many women I was meeting. Much like a Doctor, I kept a "file" on each of them with notes such as "She said this, I said that." I felt that this was necessary because if one of them happened to call me out of the blue, I could refer to her file, which, as I had said included a printed profile.

I spent an exuberant amount of time on the telephone talking to these women, answering and asking questions or just having trivial conversation. I went out on date after date even if I knew that the woman and I were not compatible or a perfect match. I went on dates, just to go out on dates and had spent a small fortune doing so. I'm not bragging or proud of it, but I went on more dates in a month, than many people do in a year, or perhaps in a lifetime.

Much like a white collar addict, I hid much of my online dating activities from my friends, family, colleagues and coworkers, even from the women I was actually dating. If I had met a woman and began to date her on a steady basis, I told my friends that we had met at a bar or at a party or something along those lines. I didn't want anyone to know that I was meeting women through online dating. If you knew some of my friend, especially my guy friends, you would understand why . . . they can be brutal!

On a few occasions, I did come out of the closet, so to speak, about my online dating and told some of my married friends. They got such a kick out of it, looking at it as a really fun hobby. They didn't understand why I was doing it, but couldn't wait to hear about the women I was meeting and about the dates, particularly the dates that you will read about in the chapters of this book. I think that many of my friends began to live out their fantasies through me and my activities. But, my hobby had become a full-scale addition.

There was a period of time when I was on so many different dating websites and going on so many dates that my monthly bills exceeded my rent. I realized that, in one-year, I had gone on over 250 dates and my savings account was dwindling. I couldn't concentrate on work, ignored my friends, I just needed my next dating fix. I was physically and mentally exhausted and so was my savings.

Thankfully, I realized that I needed a break from dating and took some time-off for a little "self-review." What I had discovered is that I had gone out on quite a lot of dates (duh), met some fantastic women (and many of their friends) and had some really interesting experiences. I began to share my adventures with many more of my friends. The more times I shared the stories of my online dates, the more comical many of the dates had seemed, so, I thought that I should write a book and that's what I did. My stories are here to entertain you as well as hopefully impart some lessons learned. If you are thinking about doing online dating, or are already doing it, learn from my experience. Best of all, I learned about myself and realized that I was now ready to take off those training wheels I had talked about, become more selective and meet women with whom I actually felt compatible, both on and off the Internet.

Now, I know that you may be thinking, "What a looser!" I mean, I know all about the stigma associated with people who have to resort to using the Internet to find dates, much like "Personal Ads." I certainly had the capability to sashay up to the bar/gallery/bookstore, etc, say hello to a woman and start a conversation, right? Sure, but, where else can you find so many people in one place looking for the same thing as you? Online dating eliminates much of the fear of dating, such as that initial rejection we have all felt at, let's say, the bar. After all, everyone doing online dating is there because they want to meet people, putting everyone on the same playing field. It gave me confidence to talk to women and allowed me to establish my own personality.

The Internet provides us with a venue to find many things, why cannot a potential girlfriend or boyfriend, husband or wife be one of them?

I had recently read somewhere that there are over 11 million people now doing online dating. That's a lot of losers, right? Wrong! There is nothing wrong with online dating, so get that stigma out of your head. No longer is online dating for the desperate. Some of the most fantastic people I have ever met, I had met on the Internet. It is a terrific way to meet new people, for both men and women. Whether it is one of the online dating websites, or another website that considers their purpose to provide a place for networking, the Internet provides us with a venue perfectly adapted to the task at hand, meeting many, many new people, all in one place.

Online dating has been a terrific experience for me and it should be for you too. And best of all, I can tell you from my own experience that it works. You can find exactly what you are looking for. Just keep in mind, as they often say about many things, you will get out of it, what you put into it. By that, I mean, you will need to make it a conscience effort to commit to it, just like you would by going to those bars/bookstores, etc.

Investigate the online dating websites out there, write a terrific profile, post some really great photos, search, send email and respond. It can be just that easy to get started. You won't need to put in the kind of time I did, but you will need to make a real effort because, as they say, nothing in life comes easy. Best of all, you will learn and grow along the way.

In the following chapters, you will read about some of my experiences from the many dates that I have had. I hope that you will find the book fun, perhaps inspiring and maybe even use some of my adventures as a learning experience. Let me make it clear right now that this book is NOT meant to put a damper on dating, particularly online dating, or any person or persons. I have enjoyed all of my experiences and I hope that they will continue.

Some of these stories are astonishing, funny, some are sad and some are even scary, but I can assure you that they are real. Yes, there are people out there like the ones you are about to read about and the real trick will be to figure that out *before* you go on the date. I hope to relate to you some helpful advice as well.

One thing though. I consider myself a gentleman so if you are expecting me to tell you every time that I had "scored," you will be disappointed. However, I will say, that I have been very, very, satisfied on numerous occasions.

And, to the Internet dating critics out there, I can only say, "don't knock it, until you have tried it!"

CHAPTER 1

Amy: The Marrying Kind

Amy was one of my first dates. She was 38. Her profile said that she was an airline stewardess (it did not say flight attendant) and from her photos, I believed her. Most of her shots were of her in her airline uniform. From our email, back and forth, I also got the impression that she was a quite a "yapper," you know, someone that talks incessantly. I would soon confirm my suspicions, but, I would also find out, that was the least of the problem.

I sent Amy my telephone number in an email, and seconds, I mean seconds later, my phone rang. "Wow, that was quick," I said. She said that she had been online and thought that she would just call. This sounded reasonable to me; after all, I was online too and have made calls that smacked of desperation as well.

Our initial conversation seemed normal enough as well, she didn't seem desperate. Amy was easy to talk with; the chit-chat was pretty much standard stuff. We talked about backgrounds, family, jobs and the like. Amy seemed pretty down to earth and I thought that we should meet. She agreed.

At the risk of sounding lazy, whenever possible, I tried to plan my dates close to my home. I did this for several reasons. But in short, if things were going really well, I thought that it would better be for her to come home with me, you know, "home court advantage." Honestly, it was not my prime objective but hey, I'm a single guy with a normal libido and the thought of consenting sex was certainly appealing. Otherwise, if the date wasn't going so well, I could make a quick escape without a lot of effort.

Amy and I had met at one of the new, hip hotel bars in Manhattan. We had drinks and appetizers and enjoyable conversation. And yes, Amy was a "yapper." She could talk about anything and everything. I know that many women have the capabilities of changing the conversation quickly, but this was a skill that Amy had clearly mastered. I had difficulty keeping up with her. We shot from one subject to another and if not for the fact that I was sitting, I would have gotten dizzy. It felt much like an "extreme date" but I actually had a good time. She was funny, good looking and asked to see me again, I had agreed to do so.

At the time, I was running a division of a large clothing manufacturer. I usually got to the office before most of my staff which gave me time to have some coffee, read and respond to email and plan my day. That day was full of meetings and conference calls, maybe a bit more than usual as I was also planning for a board meeting.

That morning, I arrived at my office as usual and began my morning routine. I switched on my laptop and sat down with some coffee, ready to check my email. To my surprise, my inbox included an email from Amy. The subject line read, in capital letters: HERE

ARE THE TOP FIVE REASONS WHY I HAVE TO MARRY YOU IMMEDIATELY!

I thought it was very funny, you know sort of Letterman like. I began to hear that Letterman drum roll in my mind and had expected to read a hilarious take from our date or earlier conversations. I quickly clicked open the email.

As I started to read, I began to get a very bad vibe. It outlined her top five and here is how it read:

1. I am the oldest of four girls and all of my sisters are married and have kids.
2. My little niece always asks why Aunt Amy isn't married.
3. My co-workers are always talking about their husbands and asking me when I am going to get married.
4. My father paid $8000.00 for my wedding dress (see attached) and it cannot be returned.
5. I promised my grandmother that I would be married before she dies; she is now on her death bed.

I still wasn't really sure if this was meant to be a joke. I mean, we had one date, how could it be real, her telling me that she wanted to marry me, and immediately. She really couldn't have been serious, could she? I thought for a moment that maybe she was pregnant; we didn't have sex, just one [first] date so if she was, it wasn't going to mine. Maybe she had some kind of immigration issue? Couldn't be, she was born and raised in New York. Was it financial problems? She had a great job. Some kind of trust fund clause? From what she had told me, I know that her family had money, but certainly not the kind that could lead to inheritance problems like this. I racked my brain over and over, and the only thing that I could come up with was that this smacked of *desperation*.

As the email had mentioned, included was a photo of Amy wearing a wedding dress. After I had clicked on it, I started to get a really, queasy feeling and could feel all of the blood rush from my face. I knew that this was not a joke. I was literally stunned.

My assistant got to the office just before nine and asked if I was OK. She said that I was "as white as a sheet," didn't look very well. I was visibly upset but I didn't tell her about the email, rather, I thought that I had a virus and asked her to cancel my meetings for the day. I closed my door and didn't want to leave my office, not even to use the men's room. My assistant ordered lunch for me so I wouldn't need to go out and I just sat there and kept running the conversations I had with Amy through my mind. I couldn't recall anything that seemed off, or even where we talked about the subject of marriage like this. I couldn't concentrate on my work and got absolutely nothing done. Unless I did something, and quick, I wasn't going to do a very good job on a major presentation that I had to finish for the board meeting, let alone managing my daily business.

For a brief moment I even thought about just blowing this off, going to the gym and work out like I was training for the Olympics. Perhaps a long walk, get a drink or even have a smoke. But the more I thought about it, I knew that I needed to handle this one, I couldn't just let it go. I had to find out where this woman was coming from and if she was for real. By this time it was about 3PM and I had decided that I needed to call her, and now.

"Hello Amy, this is Darren." After some pleasantries, I continued. "Got your email and must admit that I was as a bit shocked. I mean, I guess that finding the right girl and getting married may be the ultimately goal, but certainly not *immediately!*"

Amy was clearly upset. After what sounded like mumbling and little sobbing, she simply said, "Well mister, if that's the way you feel about it, just forget it!" She slammed down her phone, hanging up. I felt somewhat sorry for Amy but I must admit that I was relieved. What ever issues that she had, I really didn't want to know.

A guy friend of mine, a psychologist, said that Amy sounds like someone that needs help, duh! Now, you know that you don't need to go to medical school to figure that out. He toyed with the idea of having me give her telephone number to him but said that it might be considered unethical. We both simply decided to let it go and hopefully she will get help.

From what I had described, he also said that she could turn out to be a "stalker." He asked me, "You didn't tell her where you live, did you?" Holy shit . . . I really don't recall!

CHAPTER 2

Nina: Serial Dater

Nina was a serial dater. I didn't know it when we first connected but I found out quickly after we had met.

She seemed to be very organized. Nina was a sales rep and wrote all appointments in her book. If it wasn't in the book, she said, it wasn't an appointment. I knew this from our initial telephone conversation, where after a brief chat we had decided to meet at 7:00PM for a drink. She said that it would need to be a quick drink because she had things to do later that evening. Nina's parents were in town, she said, so I assumed that she wanted to spend time with them. I had suggested that we might find a better time, but she said that it was fine.

One thing that had attracted me to Nina was that she seemed down to earth and had a sense of order. Her profile said that she knew what she was looking for and would, as she put it, "Know it when I find it." This was somewhat refreshing, a bit different from some of the experiences I had previously. Several of the women I had met seemed to be just going through life, simply taking things as they come. As a matter of fact, I felt that a number of the women I had met were simply looking for a man, *any man.* I don't mean to seem derogatory here but to me, it is somewhat sad. I mean, there were some women that wanted to see me again, even though we both knew that we weren't a good match. Sure, you could go with the philosophy that two people need to get to know each other, but damn, sometimes I think that the incompatibility is clear, almost in back in white. But Nina seemed to be interested in taking the time to find exactly what she wanted and not settling for the first person that came along. I wasn't in a hurry either.

Nina was an entertainment attorney, representing a large television broadcasting company in town as her primary client. Knowing that, and also from hearing her talk during our initial telephone conversation, I could tell that her training in law had led her to be very meticulous and methodical, almost to the point of being anal retentive. I recall getting one email from her with so many questions that I wrote back, "Let the inquisition begin! . . . . LOL." Thankfully though, she took it as the joke it was meant to be. But in addition to her sense of humor, Nina was not pompous about her success. On the telephone she said that she was very fortunate to come from a good family, had a good education and great job, something that many people take for granted. But, I must admit, I wondered if I was going to "make the cut."

We had met at Café de Artes on the Upper West side of Manhattan. Artes, as it is affectionately called by locals and "foodies," is a great "date place." It is expensive, but excellent, which is probably why it has been there for many years. The food is fantastic and they have a great selection of wines, by the glass. As a matter of fact, I had found my favorite wine there several years before. There are tables situated in some of the many "cubby holes" and it can be quite romantic, under the right circumstances. We had both been to Artes before and that also gave me some comfort that we were on the same page, perhaps compatible. We had agreed to meet at the bar for a glass of wine.

Nina gave a very noticeable (and audible) sigh of relief when we first met. She said that she was happy that I looked just like my photos. As a matter of fact, she said that I looked *better* than my photos. This gave me a bit more confidence as it seemed that I had passed another one of her "tests." The "interview," I thought, was going to go well.

Looking like one's photos was important to her because she said that many guys, in her experience, post photos that are old, such as jocks then, but now carry a rather large beer belly. The same was true for some of the women I had dated as well. I know that this is a "trick" that many people do when online dating, something that I think is foolish. I mean, if you eventually meet the person, what do you expect to happen when you do?

Nina mentioned that the guy from "her last date," looked so different from his photos that she actually walked out, furious about what I had just described. As she began to elaborate on the story, I had thought that I heard her say, "this afternoon." I let it go, at first, because when we spoke on the telephone she had also said that her job kept her quite busy, leaving her little time for a social life. Perhaps I was just mistaken.

Forty-five minutes had passed and Nina mentioned that she had another appointment. She said that the "guy" that she was meeting was also an attorney. I recall that she had mentioned that her parents were in town and just assumed she was going to see them. But Nina said that she had another date at 8:00. Is it me, or is that kind of rude? She could have, at least, lied. From what I have been told (and you didn't hear this from me), many lawyers do.

I had to dig a bit more into this with Nina and she had no compunction to tell me that I was her *second* date of that evening. It seems that the guy from her story, on whom she had walked out, was her "6 o'clock" and the guy she was leaving to meet was her "8 o'clock." I was her "7 o'clock."

To her credit, Nina did say that she didn't feel that we were a match. I didn't necessarily disagree but, as we were leaving, it occurred to me, what would she have done if we had really hit it off? She responded by telling me that she would have simply blown off her 8 o'clock. I told Nina that it seemed kind of sad to me, that she would approach her dating in such a way, to which she shot back, "LOOK, I'm just trying to find a husband and I'm going see as many people I can each day until I do!"

The only question I have is, "To whom is she billing all of those hours?"

CHAPTER 3

Celia: In search of Germans

Meeting Celia was going to be fun. Her profile said that she was a segment producer for one of the major movie studios. Her specialty, I would learn, was arranging freelance hair and make-up artists for actresses before the shooting, often in their homes, and also while they were on-the-set. On the telephone, she told me stories about getting panic calls from uptight celebrities.

One story she told me was about a celebrity that was always running so late to get to the studio that in order to make up the time, the freelance artist had to often finish doing the hair and make up while the actress was sitting on the toilet. We were able to tell each other those kinds of stories on the telephone because we both seemed to be comfortable very quickly, or, metaphorically, "spoke the same language." Perhaps I spoke too soon.

Celia had a great sense of style, the type of style that I love in women; jeans and heels. I could tell that she was in a creative business because her photos were very well done. The written part of her profile was right-on, also because from the photos, she looked great in her jeans as well as that "little black dress." Her profile also said that she was about the same age as me, but you would not guess that from her photos. Although, being in the "biz," I could tell that her photos were professionally done and I wondered if it was true that photos could be deceiving. But, Celia looked good.

She had also written in her profile that she had lived "overseas" for awhile attending school and working. Not to demean her vocation, but she was intelligent, had a degree in English Literature, and it would seem to me that she would have a much different job. But Celia said that she loved the business because she was able to travel throughout the world and meet lots of interesting people, more than she would, let's say, working at the library or in publishing.

On looks alone, she seemed a better fit for show business. Celia wasn't what you would expect from an English Lit major. Now, I'm not saying that there aren't any good looking librarians or editors, but she seemed to have a creative flair more appropriate for the Arts.

Celia had, I found out later, attempted to perform in front of the camera but realized that it wasn't going to be her field. I was pleasantly surprised that she was able to come to that conclusion on her own and accepted the decision to give up on that end of the business. Not many people attempting to get into show businesses come to that point of reality. Just take a look at the so called talent and reality shows on television today.

Our date was going to include drinks and dinner. I was comfortable with suggesting dinner because I figured that even if this wasn't going to work out between us, she still was a very interesting woman. I wanted to hear more of her stories.

The restaurant we had picked was an *avant garde* place on the West Side of Manhattan, called the "The Rocking Horse." It seemed to be fitting for a place to meet Celia, as I had mentioned, she was kind of Artsy and had never been there before. I knew that she would enjoy it.

Typical of the many NY hotspots, we had to wait a long time for a table. But, standing at the bar area, we figured, would give us time to meet, have a drink and start a nice conversation. We were both drinking wine so we had ordered a full bottle, figuring that we would finish it at our table. Other did I know that we would never did get to that table.

Celia was what many guys, including me, would call, a "knock-out." She looked much younger that her 43 years of age and I had even commented that she could pass for 35. It made her blush, but she seemed to appreciate the comment.

I mentioned that Celia spoke several languages. As a matter of fact she said that she worked for a short time as a translator at the UN a number of years ago. Celia was great at making conversation and I had found it easy to talk with her. We swapped stories, mostly about work and family, and the time seemed to pass rather quickly. The date was going well.

It became clear that we were going to wait much longer for a table so we had decided to order some appetizers and have dinner at the bar if space opened up. It finally did.

As we sat at the bar having dinner, Celia began to tell me a story about her experiences in Germany where she had lived for a number of years. She had lived with a German guy and although I don't recall what she said that he did for a living, she said that he had a very good job. She loved his family and she said that they loved her as well. She had expected to get married to the guy and stay in Germany but relationship problems had started to move them apart. Celia moved back to the US with hopes to someday return to Germany, a country that she truly loved. Unfortunately, I wasn't German.

She told me that although I looked, and could even pass for a European, I was not a "German man." This was going to be a problem, she said, because she was looking to meet a German man with whom she could get serious and move back to Germany and I didn't fit the criteria.

Celia was very serious about this and told me that she even spends time at local social clubs, German restaurants and attends functions in areas of the City where there is a heavy German population. She told me that she often asks passersby [men], in German, *Wie viel Uhr ist es?* (What time is it?) in order to determine if they were German. To me, this was somewhat weird, but even more so, Celia was Jewish and related stories of her family background and the Holocaust. On that alone, I would think that German people would not be her favorite, but hey, who am I to judge?

I told her that if I had been looking for someone German, I might be looking in let's say, Düsseldorf, as opposed to the streets of New York. Besides, I would think that my slight New York accent (particularly after a few glasses of wine) would have given her a clue. Then again, I guess that I had forgotten to mention that I am Italian-English.

CHAPTER 4

Nancy: Don't Be Late!

There I was, sitting at the bar at the designated time. I would have thought from our initial telephone conversation that I was dealing with someone really, really prompt. But nooooooo.

Nancy was a "blue blood," coming from a family with old world money. We spoke on the telephone for about thirty minutes. I think that I made the initial contact by leaving my phone number. When Nancy called me, she seemed as though there was no real reason for her to be doing Internet dating. She spoke about growing up in a big house from fancy Boston suburb, schooling at Vassar and wealthy father and ex-boyfriend.

She skied, traveled throughout Europe, first-class, of course. Nancy was good at playing a snob, but I really think that she was just a "Wanna-be," now living on the Upper East Side of Manhattan.

When Nancy and I had spoken, she had mentioned that she had decided to try Internet dating, much like me, because she was tired of the bar scene. But to me, from our conversation, she just seemed like a spoiled little rich girl trying a new experience. I wondered why she just didn't stay in that Boston suburb. As I had said earlier,

I had gone out on dates even when I knew that we were not a good match, this was going to be one of those dates.

Nancy and I had discussed meeting for a drink one evening the following week, but, she said that she had one major pet-peeve. She said that if we did meet, and she wanted to be very clear about this, I would need to be "on-time" and that she wouldn't even wait for five minutes if I was late. I needed to meet this babe.

We had decided to meet at 7:00PM (sharp) at a restaurant/bar on the Upper East Side for drinks.

On the day of the date, I started to get nervous, something that I hadn't experienced before. I even thought about why I was wasting my time, but I just kept telling myself, *training wheels*. I figured, what's the worst thing that could happen? So, I got off work and went home, took a shower, shaved and changed into one of my better suits. I wanted to be sure that I was "presentable." I looked damn good.

It was a cold day and an even colder night. In New York, with car/taxi traffic, subway delays and many other reasons, you can never count on a sure commute time so I left my apartment at about 5:30PM. I figured I that would get up to the East Side and mosey around if I had to, which is what I did.

I had more that an hour to kill and I had decided not to start drinking. I wanted to hit this date with a clear head. It was one of my first post-divorce dates so I figured I had better go without alcohol on my breath. I walked in and out of the many stores that were still open, making small talk with the sales girls. I even spent time "shopping" in Duane Reade, a big New York drugstore chain. I stopped to look at things that I would normally walk by without a care. I read labels and even did price comparisons. I learned that I could buy a large bottle of Duane Reade laundry detergent for the same price as one of the leading brand.

What the hell was I doing? Is this what my social life had come to? I was comparison shopping laundry detergent while waiting for a date? Now I really did feel somewhat like a loser.

The restaurant she picked was more local bar than restaurant. It was a small Mexican place that had a larger bar area than it did tables. I pretty much knew the location and layout because I walked by it earlier while doing my pre-date mosey. I supposed that it would do for what I didn't expect to be such a banner date and I certainly wasn't expecting to get "lucky."

I went through the door at exactly 7:00PM. Except for a table of about four adults with a couple of kids, the place was empty. No one was at the bar, and more notably, no Nancy. What the heck, I figured that she would along soon, so I sat down at the bar and ordered a drink.

As many of you know, it's usually a good idea to be friendly to the bartender, so I struck up a conversation with the guy. I think he was the owner's son. I told him I was meeting a "friend" for drinks, about the time I had spent in Mexico on business and other small talk. By this time it was about 7:25, still no Nancy and I was on my second drink.

My phone rang a little after 7:30. Without an apology, Nancy started saying that she was on the telephone with her mother from Boston and needed to calm her down. Apparently, a store clerk at Loehmans in Boston had been very rude to her mother while she was trying to make a return. She said that her mother was devastated by the experience and vowed never to shop in Loehmans again. I didn't say what was really on my mind, just "how terrible," as I rolled my eyes around. I mean, how could a store clerk be so rude to Nancy's mother? I was beginning to lose patience with this gal. Still no apology, she said that she lived around the corner and would be there in about five minutes.

A little bit after 8:00, that's right 8:00, Nancy walked into the place. I recognized her from her profile photo. No apology for being late, she simply said hello, sat down and ordered a drink. She continued to expound about how rude the store clerk had treated her mother. Nancy looked like her photo, to me, just a spoiled little rich girl, guess she didn't feel the need to be the least bit courteous for being so late. I was finishing my third drink.

As Nancy continued her run down of her mom's experience, I had to stop her. I said, "Nancy, you know this is never going to work out. I mean, you know how you said that you cannot stand people who are late? Well, I have a pet peeve too. I hate people who say they hate people who are late, and then are late themselves." Then I told the bartender, "My drinks are on her." I put on my coat and started to walk out and will never forget the look on her face, but thought, now she can call her mother and they'd have a real issue to talk about.

As I was walking out, I told Nancy to "Get a life." I hope that she did.

CHAPTER 5

Maddy: Sucker Punch

With Maddy, I broke one of cardinal the brules. That is, *never, ever* meet one of my online dates at the local bar where I hung out, at least until I got to know them. Yes, I tried to stay close to my neighborhood, but I would not bring them to "my place." I simply thought that it would be awkward (at least for me) if I ran into a prior date sometime later, particularly if things did not work out. I wouldn't want her to become a regular at the place where I felt most comfortable, otherwise I'd have to find a new place.

Maddy looked nothing like the photo in her profile, I mean, it was her, but she just wasn't representative of the profile photo she had posted. First of all, she was considerably heavier, so I assumed that the photo was quite old and, her hair was cropped very short and was many different colors. Think: Punk Rocker from the '80's.

When I first got to the bar, there were a few people in the place. A few were seated at the bar and a woman sitting at a table reading. I sat down at the bar and told Randy, my favorite bartender that I was waiting for my date. I didn't tell him that I had met her online; he would have never let me live it down. What I didn't know was that there was about to be something a lot worse to live down.

As I sat at the bar watching the door waiting for Maddy, the woman from the table tapped me on the shoulder and asked if she could have the potato chips that were complimentary. Without much of a glance, I gave them to her and she went back to her table. Soon she returned and asked if I had seen one of the new exhibits at MOMA in New York. I got the impression that she wanted to have a conversation, but I was waiting for Maddy. I simply told her no and then, she asked if I was Darren. Turns out, this was Maddy.

I didn't ask Maddy why she didn't acknowledge me when I first walked into the place, perhaps she was embarrassed or just wanted to "size me up." But, it took all I could to do to keep from looking at Randy or several of my friends, who had arrived by now. I could hear the chatter at the other end of the bar, this was not going to be pretty, trust me on this one.

It was clear, real clear (at least to me and everyone else in the place), that Maddy and I had not been a match. But listen, I had agreed to meet her and figured that I should make the best of it, have a few drinks and learn from the experience. Plus, I really didn't want Maddy to cause a commotion, which would have made my next few visits to the bar much worse.

We actually did have some things to talk about. Maddy was a talent agent and I was interested in hearing about her business. She told me about her agency and a number of the celebrity clients that she represented. I am also into Contemporary Art (it said that on my profile) and she described the new exhibit she mentioned earlier. I said that I would get there to see it some time soon. I put up with this for as long as I could but wondered when this was going to end. I really did not like this girl and was hoping that she would leave.

I really don't recall how long we had talked, but I could see that Maddy was finally ready to leave. Then she asked if I wanted to go back to her place. That's probably a question that under normal circumstances, most guys would love to hear. But in this case, there was no way in hell I was going to go to her place. I told her, thanks but no. Maddy wanted to know why.

Now, I wanted to be diplomatic, but after several Vodkas, on-the-rocks, I told her that we were not compatible and simply said, "Look, you are East Village and I am West Village, this is not going to work out." I thought that it was funny, at least at the time, but I could see that my smart-ass answer didn't quite sit very well with Maddy. She retorted, "Do you know what's wrong with you man?" And before I could respond, she said, "You need to lighten up!" and, at the same time, hurled one into my gut. She had a hell of a punch and had it not been for the guy sitting next to me, I would have landed clean on the floor.

As you could imagine, my friends from the bar where unrelenting. From the beginning of this night, I realized that I had made a mistake and was going to suffer the consequences of breaking my own rule. I knew that the ribbing that I would take from them was going to last a long time. I (and they) would eventually get over it, but figured I should stay out of the place for awhile, at least until they forgot about it. They eventually did.

By coincidence, I saw Maddy several months later, yes, she was in "my place." She had lost weight and had changed her hair style, she looked much better than she did previously. We said hello and had a pleasant, but brief conversation, neither of us held any grudges. I wished her well and then she was off. Thank god, Randy wasn't on duty that night, but I was glad to see that Maddy was doing well.

CHAPTER 6

Sandy: World Series

My New York Yankees had clinched the American League playoffs. It was a terrific time to be a Yankee fan. One could only dream about scoring tickets to a Series game at the Stadium and I had assumed that about 50,000 other fans had the same dream, because unless you were willing to shell out thousands of dollars to one of those persistent, "field ticket agents" (scalpers) to sit in the bleacher seats, you didn't have a prayer. I didn't have a prayer either, so I thought.

I met Sandy at one of her Company's parties. She was an event planner and dealt with many of the mega real estate developers, architectural and interior design firms that were opening new buildings and hotels around Manhattan. I had previously read about a few of these parties, which generally read like a who's who in Manhattan society and celebrity. Other than paying them to be there, I wondered why and how they got them to come to these parties, but I've read some of the biggest name that had attended these functions; names like, Robert Dinero, Dustin Hoffman, Julia Roberts and of course, the top fashion models like Iman and Cindy Crawford. I guess it was all about the PR aspect of it and unless you were connected in some way to the function, "regular folk" really didn't get the chance to rub elbows within this class.

Sandy had some of the best photos that I had ever seen in a profile. They were not taken by a professional photographer (I found that out later), but they had shown her in various poses, headshots and full body. Sandy was one those people that actually looks good in a photo and I would describe the photos, simply as "real-life," not staged. Sandy was a good looking woman and her photos did her justice.

In addition to her photos, she had written a terrific bio as well and her job sounded interesting, a bit artsy-creative and a bit of sales. Her firm, while not well known in New York, was up and coming in the event planning market and she was doing quite well for herself helping them become established. She wrote a bit about the type of guy she was looking for and I seemed to fit her criteria, although she didn't quite fit mine. But Sandy, I would soon learn, was an *excellent* salesperson.

Sandy called me in response to my initial email one evening when I had just gotten home from work. In my early days of online dating I was bold (or just stupid) enough to give out my telephone number in my initial contact email. At that time, I figured that it would demonstrate that I was real, and serious about dating. Other than a few cases, such as several that I write about in this book, I really didn't have any problems hearing from, what I would consider to be "crazoids." Later, I learned to omit my telephone number until after I had gotten email responses and I could determine if I wanted to speak to the woman. It's not much, but I think you can get *some* insight into the Psych from a bit of written dialogue.

Although it was a weeknight and I wasn't in my "dating mode," I thought, "What the heck" and decided to take Sandy up on her offer to meet her at the company party I mentioned earlier. I mentioned that Sandy was an excellent salesperson and I figured that we would have a couple of drinks, talk and I would head home early anyway.

Sandy was extremely social and quite the little host. I had met all of her co-workers, her boss and even a few of the celebs (minor) and guests that had attended. The party was going well, sort of running on it's own so Sandy and I were able to spend a couple of hours talking. I was having a great time and Sandy asked me to hang around so that she could plan "our escape." Sandy wanted to come back to my place.

Now, as I had mentioned previously, I have been in this position before so I really didn't want to get my hopes up. But, Sandy, I later learned was also a "wild woman." She was the type of girl that put on a conservative demeanor in public but, at home, it was different story, and to me happily. And, you will note, this was our first date. I thought it could only get better from here and for awhile it did.

I saw Sandy a couple of times the following week and we both were having a great time. In one of our conversations, Sandy had learned that I was a die hard Yankee fan and asked if I wanted to go with her to "watch the Yankees in the World Series." I couldn't believe what I was hearing. Did Sandy score a couple of tickets to the Stadium?

I must admit that, at first, it was a bit of a let down, but Sandy said that she was friendly with one of the owners of the New York Sports Bar and had tickets to get in. I had just moved into a new apartment and didn't have cable yet so it was a choice of either watching the game at some local bar with the rest of the "rabble," or go to the game with Sandy. Which do you think I chose?

I was instructed by Sandy to get to the Sports Bar by 7:00PM, the game was going to start at 8:00. That would give us time to have a few drinks and hors'douveres before we sat down for dinner while watching the game.

I was excited, my friends were jealous and I was going to have a great time. Plus, I was going to watch my Yankees! I suppose that I should also mention that I was also going to watch it with a terrific, fun loving girl. In reality she really was.

Arriving at the Bar at 7:00PM brought me a bit of anxiety. I had never seen that many people trying to get into the same place at the same time. It was like Elvis had come back alive and was playing there for one night only. I wondered how I was going to get through this crowd and make it to the front door in one piece. As you can imagine, New York crowds can be very hostile, and this was the World Series with our beloved Yankees and these people couldn't get in. But, I am also from New York so I just held my breath and just pushed my way through the crowd. To my pleasant surprise, other than a few unkind words, I actually made it to the front door unscathed.

When I walked up to the door, a huge woman bouncer, and I mean huge, said, "Hey, you must be Darren." I was shocked. Not only did I not get the usual New York hassle usually associated with this type of activity, this woman actually knew my name! I had to ask her, "How do you know who I am?" She said that Sandy had described me in detail and instructed her to stand at the front door to wait for me to arrive and escort me inside to our table. I felt like royalty and knew that this was going to be a great night.

The place was packed, standing room only. It had five, huge, movie theater size screens, you could see the game from anywhere in the place. The bar area was the most packed, but I knew that we had a table.

As we walked over to the table, the bouncer said, "I'll take you to your table and then I'll go get *them*." I had to stop her, "What do you mean *them?*" She looked a bit like she had just said something she shouldn't have and simply said, "Hey, my job was to get you into the place, not give you the guest list."

The table was huge. It was like one that you might find in a company lunch room, set up in what I had expected to be "communal style." I figured that Sandy and I would simply be sitting with other people. Not a problem for me, I guess that I was just a little surprised. Besides, I was going get to watch my Yankees!

I sat down and ordered a drink while I waited for Sandy. The pre-game show was on so I had something to keep me occupied. A short time later, I was quite surprised at what I saw. Sandy was walking over to the table with, what I can only describe as, "a sea of guys." In her defense, she also had two of her girlfriend from work, but everyone else was a guy, and she knew all of them.

Sandy began to introduce me to everyone, all "the guys." She said, for instance, "This is Pete, I met him last month. This is Frank, he and I have known each other for a few years," and so on. When the introduction was finished, I had to ask her, "Who are all of these guys?" She responded by saying, "They are all my *boyfriends*."

I was stunned and it felt a little like I was on candid camera, but I had a choice. I could leave, or I could sit there, eat, drink and watch the game. I did mention that it was The Yankees in the World Series, right? Of course I stayed! And, I actually had a great time and should note that the Yankees had won, it was a thrilling game.

Sandy asked me if I wanted to see her again, perhaps the next night. During the game she told me that she was actually *seeing* all of these guys. I thanked her for a terrific night and told her that I would find a way to say thanks (I was thinking a nice gift) but that I wasn't into the group thing. She understood and said that she understood and we parted as friends. I didn't expect to hear from her again.

One night, about a month later, I had gotten a call from Sandy. I thought that it was to thank me for the gift I had sent her, but she asked that I meet her at a bar downtown, she had something to tell me. She wouldn't tell me over the telephone. I cannot tell you what was going though my mind, but I had agreed to meet her.

When I got downtown to meet her, she told me that she was getting married. She had met a guy, was in love and moving to New Jersey. OK, I knew the girl but I was bit confused and I asked, "Why did you need to meet with me to tell me this?" To which Sandy responded, "I am meeting all of my *boyfriends* to tell them." I told her thanks, but "I'm not one of your boyfriends," and wished her well.

CHAPTER 7

Serena: Whips & Chains

I should have known just from her profile photos. You'll get the picture in just one word, "Leather." On top of that, her profile name was "Skin999." Hey listen, I'm not naïve and I was intrigued. To tell you the truth, I really, really, needed a one-night stand. But, although I knew that this wasn't going to be your average, "run of the mill date," I had never expected anything like this.

Serena wanted to meet at Crobar, one of the hot local clubs in town. She said that it was one of her favorite places and knew that we would have a good time there. She had a very sexy voice but as I thought about it, her voice was more "normal," when I initially called. She answered the phone saying, "Hello," in a regular voice and seemed to change it to a more sexy voice when she realized that it was me. I blew it off because Serena sounded very uninhibited and I must admit that I was turned on. Now, I'm not really a club kind of guy, but I am a pretty good dancer, so I decided to go.

While standing in line outside the front door waiting to get in, the voice inside my head just kept saying, "this isn't your scene, this isn't your scene." But, I blew that off too.

After the prerequisite waiting game that comes along with the clubbing scene, the doorman finally let me in. The place was packed and jamming. Everyone in the place seemed to be having a great time. I knew what she looked like from her photos but I wondered how in hell I was going to find her in this place. I mean, it was "standing room only," and you just about had to fight your way to get to the bar, which I did.

As I looked out on the dance floor, I saw Serena. There was a "team" of guys dancing around her and it was quite a sight to watch. They looked like a group of male dogs surrounding a female in heat. She was a terrific dancer and I must admit that my mind was wandering with thoughts of later on that night. Everyone in the place was watching her (even the women) and I couldn't wait to meet her.

Her dress was black and "slinky." I'm not sure if slinky is a real fashion term, but to me, it was slinky. She had on high heels that I had only seen in magazines and she looked fantastic. The dress hugged the curves of her body (which was killer, by the way) and her hair was long, dark and her makeup looked as though it was applied by a team of Max Factor professionals.

Serena recognized me right away. I didn't know if she was really excited to see me, or if she just wanted to blow off the groupies that had attached themselves to her but when she saw me, she made me feel like a sailor returning home from months at sea. And I really have to tell you, I felt like a sailor returning home from war. For some reason that night I was full of self confidence. I looked good, but she was hot, dressed really sexy and I figured that if I "played my cards right," I was going to have a great night.

I do like to dance but no time in my life did I ever dance so much. Serena and I seemed to click on the dance floor, I felt her every move and she mine. I felt like we were constantly in the spotlight and at the risk of giving you the impression of "a modern Saturday Night Fever," people seemed to get out of our way as we danced. I also wasn't naïve, I knew that they were looking at Serena, but you know what? I didn't care. I was having a fantastic time. Plus, I was more popular, although I knew that it was because of this "Wingwoman." It seemed like a dream because not only was I there with a beautiful woman, having a great time, I actually had women coming up to *me* to chat. I had read about this phenomenon but had never experienced it. For a moment I even thought that if this didn't work out with Serena, I might hire her, just to come out with me.

Serena was also easy to talk to. She ran an Art Gallery in town and seemed to love her job. She was an extremely positive person and seemed to be full of life, I got that just from her dancing. I didn't mention it earlier, but she was about fifteen years younger than me. Was this going to be a short-lived relationship?

The club was trying to close and it was now very late. Serena and I decided to go out for some breakfast before we went back to "her place." Usually by this time of the morning I was off in dreamland but I was full of energy. I didn't have but a few drinks (with all the dancing, there wasn't time) and had a full dinner so I wasn't trashed.

We went to one the nearby all-night New York Diners, our conversations continued. The fact that there was such a spread in our age didn't seem to make any difference, or at least that's what

I was telling myself. We seemed to have a great time and I felt like a young club-guy again. Serena made me feel that way, she knew it too. We ate breakfast, talked and decided to head to her place, I was getting excited. The night was about to culminate in what I had hoped for, a night I wasn't going to forget.

Since our first telephone conversation, talk at the club and then at the diner, Serena didn't seem to want to talk about her photos, you remember, I called them Leather. But I was blinded by the visions of whips & chains in her closet, again, a night I wasn't going to forget.

Serena lived in a fourth-floor walk-up in the Chelsea section of Manhattan, close to the club Crobar. It was a pretty simple place, very "country." Don't get me wrong, it was nice, but not what I had expected. I mean, a girl like Serena gives the impression that she would have fantastic artwork and more contemporary furniture. Serena also had several cats.

I didn't really care about the furnishings in the apartment, my mind was focused on what was about to happen next. Serena went to use the bathroom and left me in the living room listening to some music. I expected a sight when she returned, but not quite like this. While in the bathroom, Serena put on her robe, sweats and slippers and put a "mask" on her face. I was horrified when I saw her. Not because of the way she looked but I was extremely disappointed because it was pretty clear that I wasn't going to get any "action."

Serena apologized for "leading me on" and said that she was going back to San Francisco for a few weeks to see her family and that she was planning to move back there. She asked if I would be able to feed her cats while she was gone. You heard right, feed her cats! That is where the evening had lead to . . . feeding cats!

I really never thought that I would hear from Serena again but she called a few days later, leaving me a vmail message asking me to call her back. I did have a good time at the club so I figured that I should at least return her call. Yeah, I might have even been thinking that she was going to invite me over for what I had expected a few days before.

Once again, Serena asked me to feed her cats. I decided to tell her a little story.

I told her that I once had a friend that asked me to feed his cat.

He lived on the thirtieth floor of a high-rise building on the west side of midtown and I *hated* his cat. Is a matter of fact, I hate cats, period.

They found his cat one day; apparently it decided to *jump* from the thirtieth floor terrace. At least, that's the story I'm sticking with.

I wished her well and have never heard from Serena again.

CHAPTER 8

Kaley: Material Girl

Except for her eyes, Kaley looked exactly like Madonna. I mean, she could have been an identical twin. It was uncanny, utterly uncanny. I know what you are thinking, and yes, I will admit it, that's exactly what had initially attracted me to her. Was I about to meet the *Material Girl?*

My initial contact with Kaley was about the same as the others. First, we did the email thing, chat on the telephone and planned to meet. Kaley knew that she was the mirror image of Madonna, kind of played that up. I really didn't care, I wanted to meet her and apparently, I would soon find out, everyone else did as well.

We sat at an outdoor café on one bright, sunny day on an autumn afternoon and I thought that this was going to be interesting to say the least. This wasn't my first experience with a look-alike; I had once worked with a guy, Rick, in Dallas that looked just like Michael Douglas. When we went to lunch or dinner, he would often get hounded by other patrons, often bringing over cocktail napkins over for him to sign. He said that while it was flattering, it was also annoying, but had it down to a science, just signing and not saying a word. From our telephone conversation, it didn't seem that this would be annoying to Kaley.

I had an errand to run beforehand so we had agreed to meet downtown in Manhattan, in an area where there are a number of great little restaurants. We would just find a local place and sit for coffee. I knew that she was going to be easy to spot; I would just look for the crowd.

She wore oversize sunglasses and when she smiled, you thought that you were looking at the real thing. Her voice was a bit higher in pitch but still your mind told you that you were talking to Madonna. Guess the mind can play tricks on us when we truly believe in something. At one point, I was so caught up in all of this, that I would not have been surprised if she stood up and belted one out, such as "Like a Virgin."

From the moment we had met and began to walk over to this little cafe, you could see the stares. Crossing Sixth Avenue, a major thoroughfare, everyone, and I mean everyone, had to get a glimpse of this major star. If I was not walking and talking with Madonna, then I was walking and talking with the next best thing.

They set us up, "on the stage." That is to say, outside at one the sidewalk tables, right in front. I'm not sure that the real Madonna would have sat there, I would guess preferring more privacy inside, although, I suppose that with her celebrity it would not have helped anyway. I'm sure that when Madonna herself is in town she is barraged by people and must have the need to shun the publicity.

My god, I soon realized, this was going to make Rick in Dallas seem like an ordinary case of mistaken identity but I was not really expecting this kind of attention on that afternoon. I mean, I had visions of ending up in one of those Rag Newspapers with headlines that might of read, "Who's Madonna's New Mystery Man?" or, my photo plastered with "Madonna's New Beau." Now, I don't want to give you the impression of 'flash bulbs' at a red carpet walk, but even I had wished that I brought my camera. None of my friends would believe it without a photo. Of course, I would have told them that I went out with the real Madonna.

It was utterly astonishing to me to see just how idiotic people react to [perceived] celebrity. I mean, she was identical, but if you were really a Madonna fan, you realize that she was just another look a like.

The service at the place was impeccable, as you might imagine. We ordered Cappuccino's and they came almost immediately. Busboys were constantly filling our water glasses. I have never had so many baskets of bread brought to my table, not even at my mother's house during dinner, and she's Italian! We weren't even having dinner, just coffee. And that, I've got to tell you, kept coming as well. I drank more Cappuccino that afternoon then I had on my last visit to Europe.

Our waitress was giddy. They must have held a lottery inside to determine who was going to be our waitress because the girl seemed as though she had just won Mega Millions. She was more excited then me, and I was the date! I don't know if she was taking care of any other tables that afternoon but she gave us her undivided attention. I could have asked for something that wasn't on the menu and I'm sure that they would have made it for me. After all, I was with Madonna!

We had passersby stop to say hello. Cars and taxicabs slowed to look. There were autograph requests, crowds started to gather, lots of adoring fans. One of Kaley's "fans" even asked me, "Hey, are you somebody?" To which I said, "Yes, is a matter of fact, I am." Didn't matter though, the spotlight was not on me.

Through all of this, Kaley did her best to not seem preoccupied with all of this attention, but I think that it had gotten the best of her because she had gone inside to use the bathroom and never came back. Eventually I went in to find her and she had been surrounded at the bar by a group of her adoring fans.

I went back to the table, waited for about a half-hour, then left and never heard from Kaley again. Well, at least the Cappuccino's were, "On the house."

CHAPTER 9

Vicky: Between Worlds

I have always been interested in following my Horoscope and, on several occasions, had even gone to a Psychic, just for fun. But what I would experience on this date was going to be straight out of a "Book of Sorcery."

Vicky knew about the mystical life. Like me, I knew that she was into the stars, but I didn't know how deeply until the night we had met.

Our initial telephone conversation seemed much like many of the others, pretty standard stuff. We had spoken a number of times before we had finally met and Vicky would always want to give me a "reading" from the stars. She said that it was a hobby and I have to admit, was kind of fun. Her profile said that she was a fulltime paralegal for one of the large law firms in Manhattan and was planning to attend law school if her "other interests" didn't pan out. I just assumed that her other interests were much like many other women I had dated, you know, writer, actor, dancer . . .

We had agreed to meet at a place on the Upper West Side of Manhattan, Calle Ocho, it's a Latin American restaurant and if you go, order the Empanadas. Vicky said that she had some Cuban in her family and knew that it was going to be good. Apparently she really did.

I was running late, but I called Vicky to let her know. She said that she already had the feeling I would be late and I began to get the feeling that Vicky was playing up her ability, or should I say, hobby, for my benefit. I seemed a lot like one of my visits to a real Psychic. On one occasion, the Psychic actually told me, as I walked in, "I knew you were coming." Damn, the woman was good . . . . I didn't even have an appointment!

Her profile photos were not so up to date, but I didn't know this until we had met. I had made a point to tell you earlier that online daters should use some really good photos, apparently she didn't have any so she used a few from years earlier. It didn't really matter; she was an attractive woman, albeit older than she had said. I have had this happen a few times and learned to creatively question my potential dates about their photos. I might say something like, "Wow, that photo of you skiing is really cool. Was that this season up at Killington?"

Vicky wore a conservative business suit but could just have easily have worn a robe and carried a gauntlet full of witches brew. From the moment we had met she started in with the stuff. She said that her mother and grandmother were both clairvoyant and that she had also gotten the curse. I found that I needed to change the subject often, but she would continually go back to the subject of her hobby, even telling me that she considered doing it fulltime.

After a drink and some appetizers, she excused herself, picked up her purse and went off to the Ladies Room. Seems normal, right? But when Vicky returned, I noticed that she had changed her hairstyle and darkened in her eyes and was wearing a silk scarf with brightly colored patterns. I didn't know what to expect next. Even our waitress had gestured to the other staff to come see this.

Vicky became eerily silent, tilted her head back slightly and her eyes seemed to roll back into her head as she blinked. I would not have believed it, except for the fact that I was experiencing it for myself. Was I going to get some kind of curse?

OK, I admit it, I was actually scared and even thought about running, but all I could do was to sit there astonished by what I was seeing. When it was over, she said that she had gone "between worlds" and just gotten a "vision," we were not meant to be together. I was extremely relieved. I mean, how could I be with someone that was going to continually "channel" my every thought and throw me some kind of Hocus Pocus?

This is one date that I would not soon forget, I think about it often. But, I suspect that out there somewhere, Vicky knows this.

CHAPTER 10

Jess: Hair Everywhere

Over the next month, Jess and I went out numerous times. She was actually a terrific person. We had first met for drinks at a bar near Grand Central Station, she was on her way upstate for her sisters wedding that weekend. Jess also wanted to get married, she was older. It was wintertime and cold but Jess packed light. She didn't pack her winter coat so I had loaned her mine. It wasn't a perfect fit but it worked for her. It was also my black, dress overcoat, very expensive and I had hoped that I would see it, I mean, her, again.

Jess came from a very large family. Her father was an attorney and her mother was a stay at home mom, her grandmother also lived with them. She had six brothers and sisters and a finance degree from Cornell and while studying for her CPA, she worked at an accounting firm in lower Manhattan that specialized in foreign businesses with US holdings.

Part of her charm, I thought, was that Jess also did a considerable amount of volunteer work with several charities, particularly animal shelters in town. She loved animals, telling me that her family had a "great big house" upstate with lots of pets. I actually met Jess at one the shelters before we went to dinner one night and you could see her passion for the work. She loved to feed and care for the animals saying that it reminded her of her childhood days visiting her grandparent's dairy farm during the summers. Jess considered being a veterinarian but switched to finance because her grandparent's lost their farm for financial reasons.

To help after 9/11, the government had set up a program to grant money to businesses that had been located near the World Trade Center area. As you could imagine there were numerous businesses that would apply for the grants and from what Jess had told me, the government made it quite easy to obtain the funds. She knew this because her firm represented many of these businesses.

One evening, I noticed that Jess was agitated, I thought, over the grant process. We had numerous discussions on the subject, over the telephone and when we had met for dinner. I thought that it was a terrific program to support the businesses that were affected by 9/11, she did as well. But Jess finally confided what had been bothering her. It appeared that several of the shelters were loosing donations because many of the businesses were either closing or could no longer afford to support the cause. The shelters were becoming inundated with animals and they could not afford to care for, or keep them, many animals were being euthanized. Jess was clearly upset by this.

I had realized that I had not yet been to her apartment. Jess preferred to come to mine, which was fine with me. She lived on the Upper West Side and we had spent most of our time together downtown, closer to my apartment. You remember me mentioning the aspect of the home court advantage?

But one night, Jess invited me to her apartment for drinks. She said that she would introduce me to her "kids" and that I could finally get back the coat I had loaned here several weeks earlier. We had been dating for about a month and I was finally going to see where she lived, I must admit, it was exciting.

I was horrified by what I saw. Jess lived in a typical, small New York City apartment, you know, the type that's advertised as "cozy," meaning you couldn't spit without hitting a wall. But this wasn't the reason for my shock. It appeared to me that Jess was hording many of the animals from her shelter. She had dogs, cats, hamsters and even a parrot (in her defense I think that the parrot had already been hers). But there were far too many animals in those rooms. If she and I were going to use the bedroom, it was clear to me that we would have an audience, and many of those would have wet noses. This was absurd and I now knew why she preferred to come to my apartment as opposed to hers.

Jess opened the closet door to in her bedroom to get my coat. There was animal hair everywhere. Many of her "kids" were sleeping in the closet and my coat had a layer of hair. Not just a few hairs, I mean a layer. I wondered if it was ruined. Apparently, it seemed to me, that Jess didn't own a vacuum or know how to use one. It was utterly disgusting.

While I like animals, particularly dogs, I suggested to Jess that she might consider downsizing in that area. I mean, she seriously needed to do something about this situation; no sane person could live with this many animals, particularly in a New York sized apartment. But Jess said that there was no way that she was ever going to get rid of

Max, Icarus, Libby, Dondi, Tino, Batch, Floss, Tater, Victoria . . . and the rest, this was their new home. All she seemed to be missing was a turtle and some goldfish.

Jess wanted to see me again but I told her, as I was leaving, I wasn't the "farm" kind of guy. Besides, I didn't have the amount of "vacuum cleaner bags" that it would take to clean and maintain my clothes.

CHAPTER 11

Jolie: I am a Lesbian

For our first date, Jolie had invited me over to her place for drinks . . . the sex was great.

I could not believe that I had sex with a woman, *before* we had ever gone *out* for drinks or dinner, particularly so soon after actually meeting. It usually didn't happen that way, at least not for me. Normally my relationships (online and offline) had a certain progression to the point of sex. In my defense however, I didn't stand a chance. Jolie was sexually assertive, careful, but sexually assertive.

It's not that I did not know Jolie at all. Our email correspondences were going back and forth for quite some time. Soon, we progressed to speaking often on the telephone and this also went on for some time. I had gotten to know Jolie very well through our email and telephone conversations. She was a very open and upfront woman and I knew that she was uninhibited, it said so in her profile, I am not that naïve. I would not say that I was scared, but I had never known anyone like Jolie and this may have lead to my reluctance to actually meeting her. I thought that she might be too progressive for me.

Jolie worked as a copywriter for a publisher of children's books. She had been married previously and had three kids, all of whom lived full-time with their father, seeing her on weekends. Jolie's profile photo did not do her justice. Yes, I did say Photo, not photos, as she only had one, a headshot. This was another one of my "rules" that I was about to break. Normally I did not meet a woman if she only had one photo, I wanted to see the more of the person. This may make me sound somewhat shallow, but listen, fair is fair and my profile had several photos and they knew what they were getting, I wanted the same. There are many interpretations of petite, athletic and fit, so having more photos on a profile help to support one's said body type.

I was pleasantly surprised when I met Jolie. She had a terrific figure and a killer smile. She also had a great personality and we shared the same taste in music and wine. Jolie also had a killer apartment, with a fantastic sound system. It was loft style and by New York standards, it was quite large, with a super-sized fireplace in the area where her bedroom was located. The apartment was as sexy as Jolie was herself.

We never left the apartment that night. I mean, when she invited me over, I had expected to have a couple of drinks and then go off to someplace for a bite to eat. Jolie wanted to stay at home and didn't care how late it was getting. She wanted to drink, dance and make sure that I had a good time, she was the perfect hostess. We had both wanted to see each other again.

We had decided to go dancing for our second date. We met at one of the new clubs in the trendy Meat Packing District. It was during the week so there was no line and we figured that we would just walk in. But still, the doorman was a complete asshole. This jerk was going to make us stand there behind the velvet ropes until he was damn ready to let us in and Jolie was quickly becoming aggravated, for good reason. At one point, I expected her to pop the guy, and frankly so did he. He let us in.

For a weeknight, the club was rather busy. You can never tell with these places, the heavy action usually gets started quite late. Jolie was a night person.

At the bar, we ordered our drinks and took a look around the place, it was huge and I happened to notice that there were many couples, including men with men and women with women. This seemed to excite Jolie.

Thinking that she was joking, Jolie said that she wanted "work together," pick up another woman and head back to her place. She said that we needed to get in the center of the dance floor. She said that she would make eyes at the single women in the room and one would fall into her "trap." I laughed because I thought that she was kidding, I soon realized that she was not.

I was having another great time with Jolie. She was a different type of woman from those I had been dating. She seemed to not be bothered by much of the normal, everyday bullshit and didn't bitch about the shit that had happened in her life. She was happy with her life, she said, and seemed to take things in stride. She was refreshing and fun.

As we danced, Jolie asked, "I did tell you that I'm a lesbian, right?" You can imagine my surprise. I think I would have remembered her telling that. All I could think to say was, "You cannot be a lesbian, because we just had sex. That would mean that you are bisexual." Joile said that she did not like the word bisexual and shot back, "I am a lesbian." Jolie told me that she preferred women, but needed a man, "Every once in a while." I didn't want to be that man.

All I could think to myself was "Whatever." She was what she was and I didn't see Jolie again.

CHAPTER 12

Ina: You're under Arrest

Ina said that she was from Italy, just arrived to New York and was staying with a friend/roommate. She spoke English very well, with an accent, and said that she also spoke French, German and Japanese. She spoke some words to me in a few of these other languages, but what the hell, I didn't know better. I speak Spanish, surprisingly, she said that she didn't.

I had planned a great date. I had gotten reservations at Suenos (Spanish for Dreams) a new, TexMex, restaurant downtown. The restaurant had become very popular, I was lucky (and proud) to get reservations.

The reason Ina had moved to the US, she told me, was to further study English and learn about New York. She said that she was a travel agent and had numerous clients from Italy that wanted to visit New York. Although she had been here before, it was only for short visits and she needed to learn more about the City. Ina wanted to become a "New Yorker," and I was going to be her guide.

Ina said that she was not the type of girl to meet her dates, "at the location," preferring to be picked up at her building. She insisted that I pick her up in a "Black Limo." Was this Babe kidding me or what? I told Ina that tonight (and any other night for that matter), her "Limo," was going to be "Yellow."

From her profile I could see that Ina was quite attractive and being a sucker for cute, European accents, I decided to accommodate her by picking her up in front of her building in one of our fine, New York City taxicabs, and of course, it was yellow. How more New York could that be?

It was a Saturday morning and Ina had called me on the telephone after we had exchanged several email messages through the dating website. Usually, I had planned a "first date" for nights during the week, saving the weekends, particularly Saturday night, for women that I had already met and wanted to see again. But Ina wanted to meet that night.

At the risk of sounding like a real cad, I need to be completely honest here and tell you that I had canceled my date with another woman for that night so that I could meet Ina. I know how terrible that must sound but the date I had already planned really wasn't going to go anywhere. I mean, at least to me, it was simply going to be one of those dates that I mentioned earlier; a date, for the sake of going on a date (Besides, who wants to stay home alone on a Saturday night?) Plus, the way I figured it, if she really did like me, I would be able to see her again some other time if she wasn't too pissed off. She wasn't very disappointed when I canceled, but no, I never did see her again.

Ina was staying uptown in the Sutton Place area. Sutton Place is an expensive part of town, loaded with townhouses and the rich and famous. I needed to take a cab from downtown where I lived, pick her up in Sutton Place and then go back downtown to the restaurant. I had assumed that I would need to take her back uptown after our date as well. She said that she would meet me downstairs in front of her building.

I knew the building. It was a large co-op and I had a friend that had lived there. As I drove up in the taxi, I saw her. Ina was a "vision." She stood right out front, under the entrance awning. She was one of the most beautiful women that I had ever seen. From her profile photos I knew what she had looked like, but I have got to tell you, I was really impressed. Was this a dream? The cab ride was worth it and I couldn't wait to walk into this restaurant with her.

Naturally, we would need to wait for our table. I was okay with that, Ina was gorgeous and the looks from the other patrons (men and women) made it worth the wait. Ina was a "head turner," and yes, "men are dogs" and that night would support this cliché because the drooling was quite apparent. Although Ina seemed to enjoy the attention, she also was sure that they (the dogs) knew that she was with me. Shaw okay with public display of affection.

Ina was dressed in a tight fitting mini skirt (stylish, not cheesy) and her legs were fabulous. I figured that Ina had plastic surgery *in all the right places* and her blouse certainly enhanced her bust size. She was about my height, but in her heels, great heals, she stood taller. I didn't know where or hoe the evening would end, but for the immediate, I was having a great time.

As an Italian woman with excellent taste, she knew good wine. I didn't even need to look at the wine list because Ina had that covered.

I didn't care (I found out later) that the bottle was $125.00. It was great wine and we were having a terrific dinner.

While having desert, Ina said that she was starting to feel "ill." At one point, she actually doubled over, resting her head on the table. I was concerned, but also got the feeling that she was a pretty good actress, her moaning seemed overkill. You could imagine my surprise when Ina said that she wanted to go to the hospital, saying, and I quote, "You must have poisoned me."

At that point, I knew that there was something rotten happening here. I mean, she may have been ill, but the hospital? My stomach was beginning to knot and I needed to do some quick thinking. We jumped in a cab and Ina kept repeating over and over in her best moan that she wanted to go to the hospital. But, I whispered to the driver to take us to Sutton Place, but I told Ina that we were going to one of the better hospitals uptown.

Ina's building was located just off the Queensboro Bridge, a major in and out roadway for Manhattan. From my experience in the area, I remembered that the NYPD often sets up a major check point there to look for "suspicious characters" coming into and leaving Manhattan. I considered Ina to be a suspicious character.

As we approached the building, Ina realized that we were not going to the hospital and became angry, almost to the point of being violent. We pulled up in front of her building and thankfully, the NYPD was in full force. Before the taxi had stopped, I rolled down the window and yelled over to one of the officers standing on the outside of his police car and he began to walk over toward the cab. The second we stopped, I grabbed Ina by her arm and literally had to pull her from the car. This was going to be an exciting night for the NYPD and one that I would never forget.

The officer and his partner came over to us and I quickly explained what was happening. Ina said that she was felling much better and wanted to leave, but the police had detained her and soon she was surrounded by a group of New York's finest to see what was happening.

I told the officer that I had picked her up in front of the building earlier, went to dinner and shortly thereafter she had accused me of poisoning her, insisting that I take her to the hospital. Yes, he said, it sounded suspicious and we went into her building to see the doorman. He said that she did not live there but has been seen standing in front of the building regularly, like she was waiting for someone. The doorman came outside where they were holding Ina and made a positive ID; one would not forget having seen Ina.

Ina and an accomplice were arrested.

Apparently they had a long list of arrests in such places as Monaco, the Virgin Islands and the Riviera. Their crimes were international and their MO, it was explained, was to find a "Mark" and in some way try to blackmail for money. In my case, the agents said that Ina and her accomplice figured that I would simply pay them rather than go through the hassle that they would put me through. Ina was from Eastern Europe and not Italy.

I had hoped that Ina enjoyed her last meal, before being confined to one of the "luxury suites" at Rikers Island.

CHAPTER 13

Candy: No Business like Show Business

Candy was proud of the fact that she was now, "a working actress." Earlier in her career she had put in her time waiting tables and was finally at a point where her living now came from doing commercials, voiceovers and off Broadway as well as stand up comedy.

She wasn't a *major* celebrity but I assume that many new actors would be satisfied with this level of stardom. Candy was very ambitious, serious about her craft and aspired to reach for national celebrity status, movies, Broadway and more.

My first date with Candy came with an invite to one of her shows. She may not have been a Merrill Streep yet, but she was certainly talented. You could see that she would get there and you would her it in her voice. Even if our relationship didn't make it, I wondered if I would some day be able to say that, "I knew her when." The show was a success and was getting very good reviews, so was Candy.

Candy was a native of Florida and went to the University of Tampa, receiving a Performing Arts degree. She said that she always wanted to be an actress and after school, like many do, she moved to New York to pursue her dream. Her family was against her decision to move to New York but after seeing her local success they knew that she should. Candy was a very good looking woman and you could see her doing well in the business.

I had previous dated other women in show business and usually, they would use any form of media, such as their online dating profile as more of a promotional piece. But Candy's profile was different. It made her seem like a normal woman, seeking to meet someone for dating and a long-term relationship. As a matter of fact, other than a couple of photos that showed her on stage somewhere, you would not know that she was an actor, simply listing her occupation as, "Self Employed."

Our initial telephone conversation had led me to believe that Candy was looking for some normality in an otherwise abnormal life. She said that she was tired of dating men from the business because they were usually quite "flitty." That was the term she used to describe someone that was undependable. I would later learn that she was describing her ex-boyfriend. What Candy was relating was different from the other show business people I had dated. I told her that it was my experience that show people seemed to flock together, I guessed, because they all understood the business. One of my previous dates even asked me if I would be able to understand when she needed to be off on the road for months at a time. Candy said that we were both on the same page, we agreed to meet.

After her show, we had decided to get some coffee. We only had a few minutes because she had an early casting call in the morning and then needed to get to rehearsal. Candy and I would meet again at The Blue Ribbon Bakery, a well established restaurant downtown that had always gotten good reviews, we had both been there. She had one night off, during the week, and that was going to be the night that we would meet again. Candy seemed like she was going to be a fun date, quite the comedian.

At The Bakery, as it is known to locals, we had a great time waiting for our table. Candy told me some jokes from her repertoire and her stand up routine. In particular, she turned her breast enlargement into a very funny skit and although I knew that she had gotten the surgery when we spoke on the telephone, they were much bigger in person.

Candy confided that she had her breast enhancement at the request of her ex-boyfriend. She said that the guy was into big breasts. They had been living together for about eight years and her career was starting to take-off, his was not. She said that she had agreed to the surgery to appease the fellow. But, as their relationship had started to wane, Candy decided that she needed to find someone that could provide a more stable home-life and still allow her to pursue her acting career. Candy was not shy to tell me that she wanted someone that was financially stable so that the "up and down life" would be a thing of her past.

It is not a large place with cozy tables. The Bakery is a terrific, two level restaurant, with several alcove tables downstairs where they actually bake their own bread. You can smell the baking from anywhere and you can also hear the conversations going on at nearby tables, particularly at the first floor tables where we had been seated.

Candy and I were having a great time. I noticed, much like me, she became funnier after a few glasses of wine. Other patrons noticed as well because the people at the nearby tables laughed as Candy talked, becoming more attentive to our conversation. The five guys sitting next to us were egging her on and she obliged, particularly after one guy claiming that he had seen her in one of her show.

Throughout her career, Candy had mentioned earlier, she had a large gay following and the guys sitting next to us all claimed to be gay. Regardless, to me, this was soon becoming a "group date," but I figured that Candy had gone there with me so she would leave with me, right?

After sharing one of The Bakery's signature deserts, I had asked for the check. Candy and I were going to one of the terrific little wine bars near my house for a nightcap, perhaps more, so I was thinking. The bathrooms at The Bakery are located on the lower level so that's where Candy was off to.

Now, most guys will tell you that women take a considerable amount of time freshening up, but after about fifteen minutes, I had decided to go downstairs to make sure that she was OK. What I had observed was somewhat comical, but, as I had been sitting and waiting, somewhat inconsiderate. Candy was moving from room to room, doing her stand up routine and singing. The patrons downstairs must have thought that The Bakery had brought in live entertainment and seemed to be enjoying it. In one room, Candy actually started to belt out an old Broadway tune, "There's No Business Like Show Business," originally sung by Ethel Merman in "Annie Get Your Gun."

Candy was "on" and working her material.

After her "set" was completed, we were leaving the restaurant at the same time as the party of five that had been part of Candy's audience earlier that evening. They had said that they were going to one of the local gay clubs in town and asked us to go with them. Candy wanted to go, I did not.

I hope that she had a good time.

CHAPTER 14

Linda: Is there a Doctor in the House?

This was our first date and Linda said that she wanted to go to Apizz (pronounced Ah-bitz). Much like me, she was a foodie and her online profile said that she also enjoyed going to great little restaurants. I had told her about this restaurant during one of our initial telephone talks and we spoke about it further when we had agreed to meet for coffee near the hospital where she had worked. Linda was a nurse and said that she really didn't drink.

Apizz is a fantastic little Italian restaurant down in the East Village and to set the stage for you, it had recently opened and like most new places in New York, it becomes quite difficult to get a table, particularly without reservations. But, I'm going to tell you my little secret for getting in such places, just as I had told Linda. Unfortunately, I told her too late and this date was going to be my own doing, or rather, my undoing.

Linda was from the Midwest and had only been living in New York for a few months. Being new to the City, she said that it was the main reason why she was doing the online dating thing; new in town and wanted to meet some new people. This is certainly acceptable, as I had said earlier it's a great way to do so. But Linda, as I had observed, was very outgoing and very social. Linda was also a lot of fun, but if you didn't know her, as many of the patrons in Apizz would soon surmise, one might consider her to be "nuts." I realize that is not a medical term or somewhat derogatory, but you'll have to give me some room here, you haven't met Linda and I haven't finished the story.

It's not guaranteed, but I have often had success getting into some of these new restaurants by calling ahead and simply saying something like, "This is Dr. James and I am only here for tonight, I would like to bring a very special *patient*." Who could refuse that and in the case of Apizz, it worked like a charm, it was a weeknight and they said to come right in and they will find us a table. I came back to the table where Linda and I were having coffee and simply told her, "Let's go." Linda was very impressed and my ego was stroked.

We met early in the evening and Linda came directly from work, she was still wearing her hospital uniform and neither of us had eaten yet. I was OK with the uniform, she told me in advance but I didn't realize until we had arrived to Apizz that it would actually support my little story to get in.

As expected, the place was very busy and I had checked in as "Dr. James," party of two. My story seemed to make sense to them, particularly since they saw Linda wearing hospital garb. One of the young women at the podium whispered a question to me, "Is that your special patient?" To which I whispered back, "Yes."

We had decided to order some wine while we sat in their waiting lounge. This is when I started to see why Linda, "didn't really drink."

It wasn't quite Kim Bassinger in "Blind Date," a movie from the 80's, but Linda seemed to become louder and louder as she drank her wine. In addition, she seemed to make a very noticeable and strange movement with hair, moving her head back and forth. Under normal circumstances this might be simply be considered odd, but the staff thought that she was a "patient." Our table was ready and the staff (and other patrons) would soon notice some of Linda's actions.

For instance, Linda asked me (Loudly) why they referred to me as "Doctor" when they seated us. When I have pulled this stunt in the past, the other person was always in on the joke. It was at that point that I had realized, this time it might just become a problem. Somewhat embarrassed about what I had done without telling her, I simple said, "They must think that I'm a Doctor, let's just keep it our little secret."

In some of the earlier restaurant reviews that had been written about Apizz, the service had been considered inattentive. But that night we were taken well care of. Linda had mentioned that they always seem to be around our table, almost to the point of neglecting the others. I had gotten deeper and deeper.

I decided that I would tell Linda the truth when we had left the restaurant. Aside from my underlying guilt, she was a very nice girl and didn't deserve to be treated like this, joke or no joke. However, as we were leaving, all of the staff wanted to say goodbye to her. In front of her, they thanked me for being the "kind of Doctor" that took such care and interest in his patients.

I never got the chance to apologize to Linda. I probably never will.

And, for what it is worth, "Dr. James" has retired from getting into restaurants.

CHAPTER 15

Marion: Puke-A-Rama

Let me tell you right up front that this wasn't an online date, rather a blind date, set up for me by one of my I-Banking buddies, Barry. I wanted to relate this story to you because for some reason, so many of the naysayers (Barry being one of them) seem to feel that blind dates are more acceptable than online dating. I found out that it isn't.

Online dating is not like getting a "mail-order bride." I mean, we all have read the stories about people (men, in particular) that buy a spouse from photos, even a catalogue. That type of activity doesn't interest me. In my experience, online dating is simply a means to meet new people and does not preclude the rest of the dating process. Again, it's no different than meeting someone at a bar. You still need to connect, meet, talk, have some level of compatibility and take it from there.

Marion was running late. I sat waiting in the "lounge area" of a very chic, downtown bar in the SoHo area of Manhattan and wondered what I had gotten myself involved in. Barry was a new friend and didn't know me very well, but after hearing about my online dating (I didn't bring it up, a mutual friend did), he thought that he should "help." He thought that Marion, whom he worked with, would be compatible with me and also wanted to prove that online dating was for losers. Barry told me that Marion was "hot." He wasn't married and I wondered why he wasn't dating her, he said that he had at one time.

Apparently, Barry misunderstood my reason for online dating. While it is certainly possible to "score," I can tell you, at least for me, it had not been my primary objective. But hey, at the time, I was in my full-scale-dating-mode and decided that I would take the chance. I mean, how bad could it be?

Marion first called me on the telephone after Barry introduced us via email. She worked for the same firm as Barry and was involved with trading commodities. She seemed intelligent and we did have some things in common. At the time, I was an I-Banking consultant, raising capital for firms interested in merger and acquisitions. If nothing else, I figured I could get through the date "talking shop."

It was about ½ hour beyond our meeting time so I figured that I had better call her. I mean, no one wants to be stood up, especially me. If she wasn't coming, I figured I had other potential dates and honestly, I was suspicious anyway. I still couldn't get over the fact that Barry was a successful guy and if Marion was a good as he said, why was he not still with her? Perhaps they just weren't compatible?

Marion answered her phone after several rings. She said that she had been drinking for most of the afternoon and I could tell that she was plastered. Is a matter of fact, she handed her cellphone to the cab driver so that I could tell him where to drop her off, because, although she knew it was in SoHo, she couldn't remember exactly where we were meeting. I suggested that we plan to meet another time, but she all but begged me to wait. She had a terrible day and said that she needed a night out.

Against my better judgment, I had decided to wait for her. I can only tell you that it was much like human nature, the desire to slow down to look when passing a car accident on the highway. But this, my friends, was going to be worse, more like a "train wreck."

Marion had been fired that afternoon from her job. She made this announcement to me immediately after she had [finally] arrived. She said that she had gone to a bar to be consoled by a friend and just started drinking and drinking. She said that she wanted to have one more drink and then go home. If we had been sitting directly at the bar, I'm not sure that the bartender would have served her, but our waitress was young and inexperienced and brought her vodka on the rocks. Hey, more in common, that's what I was drinking!

It was very difficult to speak to her. Aside from the fact that she was slurring, one sip into her drink and she ran off, or more accurately I should say, staggered off, to the Ladies Room. As soon as she came back to her chair, she was off, again and again.

We have all been there. What Marion was experiencing was the classic case of having had way too much to drink. She was vomiting and according to the waitress staff, had made a horrible mess of the Ladies Room. Apparently she didn't have very good aim either. She was also passing out.

Marion lived in New Jersey. Now, I may be a gentleman, but after all of this, I wasn't going to take her home myself. The bar staff flagged down a taxi and I gave the driver a $20 bill to take her home across the river. Thankfully one of the waitresses knew the area where Marion lived and agreed to take her home, after I left a handsome tip.

I simply felt sorry for the person that had to clean that cab.

CHAPTER 16

Carrie: Please listen to the Tape

After my first year or so, I had realized that many online dates were somewhat of a repetitive process. More specifically, many seemed much like an interview, I was answering questions from women that I had no real interest in having a relationship. They seemed to be the same questions over and over. "Where are you from? How many bothers and sisters do you have? What do you do for a living?" . . . . You get the picture.

One date actually took out a piece of paper from her purse and began to read the questions off. Had she simply wrote them to me in an email, I could have better responded. Then again, I probably would have simply deleted her from my website.

Now, don't get the impression that I was becoming less enthusiastic about online dating, I was not. But listen, I had gone on so many dates that I found the questions and answer game monotonous. My answers could easily be canned and I wondered how that might work.

But, I also knew that it was time for me to move forward and become more selective in the process, contacting and seeing the women that I really wanted to meet. I also realized that I had been spending a considerable amount of time and money on dates that were going nowhere. I had never left a date sitting there, or would just get up and leave. That wasn't in my make up.

I thought quite a bit about the idea to actually "can" some of my answers and use it in situations where it became necessary.

Carrie was one of my last, *dates just to date*. She was also, I quickly learned, a royal pain in the ass and I did not like her, at all. She was snotty, rude and pompous. And, she began yelling at me for taking so long to get back to her, as she put it, "Wasting so much time sending email to you." I think that I would have gotten a fork in the head if I told her that this was not going to work out and started to leave. However, I thought that this bitch, need to learn a lesson and then go off somewhere and grow a new attitude.

As Carrie continued her barrage of questions and insults to my manhood, I decided to use a pre-recorded tape. I told her that I was going to the men's room and told her to listen to the tape. I switched on my personal voice recorder and headed for the bathroom.

"Hi, this is Darren. I am divorced, amicably and have no children. I grew up in New York and . . ." It ended with, "If after listening to this tape, you decide that we are not a match, I'll understand if you would simply like to leave. Best of luck to you."

As I had hoped, Carrie was gone. Thankfully, she left my personal voice recorder.

CHAPTER 17

Short Dates

Many of my dates had been very short, for a number of reasons; either I didn't like them, or they didn't like me. Heck, some didn't even get to the date phase, realizing over the telephone, or in a few cases, through email, that I hadn't found my match. None the less, I've met some interesting women and wanted to tell you some of the stories associated with these adventures. Maybe I'm just being picky?

> *Eve: I'm a Musician, Fashion Designer, Writer, Producer, Singer . . .*

I can assure you that this story will be shorter than the date. To set it up, just think about Eddie Murphy, in the movie, "Coming To America." In particular, recall the one scene when he was in the bar interviewing potential mates. One of the women was quite ambitious, having a diverse idea of her talents. She wanted to be *many* things. So did Eve.

Eve had been educated in Paris, where she had lived before moving to New York. Both of her parents worked for the US government and they had moved around quite often. She had lived throughout

Europe and spoke several languages. Eve was into fashion and the Arts and wanted to make her career in these areas, and apparently, all of them.

The best part of this date had been after we actually parted, it was quite a sight. Eve had mentioned that she was off to meet a record producer and after that was going to see her agent regarding a movie, the next day was showing her designs to one of the fashion houses. I think that you get the picture.

We had met at a downtown coffee shop in the Union Square area of Manhattan. The Park itself is a magnet for a diverse mix of people and always very crowded. They come to play checkers, paint, write, skateboard or just hang out. That afternoon, they would be treated to what would seem to be a visit from a European queen.

Eve was wearing one of her designs. It was a very colorful robe with a dyed fur collar and included a matching, flat, brimless cap with a tassel. She was quite a vision and as she walked down the street, the crowds of onlookers parted as if they were in the presence of royalty.

I'll keep a look out, perhaps one day seeing Eve in the movies, or Vogue, or maybe even on MTV.

> *Andrea: Please leave . . . . NOW!*

I had invited Andrea to the Christmas party of one of my clients, BIG MISTAKE!

The party was black tie and she looked great in her evening gown. Many of my colleagues were impressed, commenting on how [hot] beautiful she was and as you could imagine, this made me feel pretty good. Andrea and I had gone out on several occasions and admittedly I knew that this wasn't going to be a long term relationship, she did as well. But, it was fun while it lasted.

At the party, which was filled with an array of my Investment Banking colleagues, Andrea let loose. She was constantly on the dance floor with anyone that had two legs and she was having a great time.

In particular, one of the older gentlemen, one of the firm's clients, seated at my table (the party included a sit down dinner) mentioned that he had his yacht docked in Miami for the season. Yes, he did say Yacht and this was music to Andrea's ears.

Shortly after dinner, the CEO (whom had hired me) and his wife had approached as I stood talking with some people in one of the other rooms of the hall where the party was held. He asked how long I knew this girl and suggested that I take a look at her on the dance floor. She was dancing "frantically" with the Yacht guy from Miami and in between songs they had a horrible case of what could only be described as "suckface."

It was embarrassing to see (imagine how I felt) and the CEO "suggested" that I ask her to leave. Andrea, they thought, was acting like one of those high priced call girls.

Andrea would not leave when I said that I would bring her home. The CEO said that if she didn't, he would have security escort her out. Things were getting ugly and it seemed that I had my hand full. Thankfully, one of the other guests and his wife were able to talk some sense into her. They said that they would bring her home in their car.

Perhaps Andrea is now dancing somewhere in Miami.

> *Sara: Christmas Dinner*

It was going to be a delightful evening. Sara had invited two of her friends, a married couple to spend Christmas with her in New York. They were from Georgia, where she had grown up and this was their first visit to New York. The woman was Sara's best friend and they had been close since high school. The Duck, which Sara had prepared, was, unfortunately, the best part of the evening.

Toward the end of dinner, the doorbell rang and in walked a guy that Sara had introduced to us as her *ex-boyfriend*, let's call him John. It was clear to me that the guy still had feelings for Sara and I really think that it was mutually.

The couple from Georgia was more stunned that I. But listen, Sara and I were not going to be long term and frankly she did me a huge favor. I had intended to end our relationship anyway and but knew that I couldn't break up with her so soon after such a delightful dinner.

I was happy for the reconnected couple, hope that John and Sara are doing well.

> *Chelle: Duck Lips*

It was short for Michelle. I saw from her profile that she was a blond haired, blue eyed, beauty, born in Greece to American parents but moved to the US when she was young. She rode her horse each weekend in Connecticut. Her profile had numerous photos of her demonstrating her equestrian ability, jumping hurdles and the like. But, I would never meet "Quincy," her horse.

Chelle listed her occupation as "Actress," but I later found out that her day job was teaching autistic children. She had a graduate degree in education, but said that her passion was acting. How could she know? I mean, other than her local church functions while growing up, she had never actually been on the stage. She said that she had gone on a few casting calls and was taking acting classes.

I met Chelle in the bar at the W Hotel in New York after work. I arrived before her, waiting while having a drink. I was startled when I first saw her.

Chelle had come directly from her Doctor, a plastic surgeon. He had injected so much collagen into her lips that she looked like a duck. I thought that she was going to get stuck to her cocktail glass. I couldn't keep my eyes off those lips and she noticed.

Our date and short relationship was quickly over.

> *Roberta: Two for the Price of One*

Roberta was going to meet me for a drink after having dinner with some of her friends. She said that she was new to Internet dating and I'm not sure that this was a real good venue for her. She said that she was somewhat shy and that she had reservations about meeting guys outside of her normal circles. Her friends, she confessed, had talked her into it posting a profile online. I must have made her feel comfortable when we initially spoke on the telephone, or so I thought, because she had agreed to meet me.

We were going to meet at a bar that she had suggested, near the restaurant where she was having dinner. She knew the area quite well. I had never been to this particular bar and thought that I should get there early. I mean, what if she got there and I had not yet arrived? From what she had told me about her reservations, I figured that she might just leave.

Other than a few people, the bar was empty. I sat down and ordered a glass of wine facing the door so that I could easily see her as she walked in. Several people came in but, no single women. A short time later two women walked through the door and one waved to me, it was Roberta. The other I did not know.

Roberta introduced me to her friend, Patricia, and *both* sat down with me at a table in the bar area. By this, I had assumed, Patricia was staying. She said that she was there to support Roberta as she was afraid to meet me alone. I really wasn't into "tag-team" dating. And besides, Roberta wasn't for me anyway, neither was her friend.

I bought the two ladies a drink and said goodnight.

> *Macey: Goldfish*

We had read each others profile and after the prerequisite email, had a short conversation on the telephone. Macey was clear that she wanted to get married again (she was divorced), heck, so did I. She had also mentioned that she wanted to start a family soon, you know, because of the biological clock thing.

She was 36 and was working for a fragrance company at one of the large retailers in town (you know, the one on Fifth Avenue). She said that she had gone on several Internet dates and was yet to find a suitable mate and from what she had told me, not sure that I actually stood a chance.

Macey was in retail and had very difficult hours so we had decided to meet for coffee near her store after lunch. She was an attractive woman with a high sense of style, dressed extremely well. She was in front of the public all day and said that her job required her to look good all of the time.

She started with her questions almost immediately, wondering why I had previously been married and did not have any children. I responded by telling her that my wife and I decided not to have children in order to concentrate on our careers. This seemed to suffice but then asked if I had a dog? I said that I did not. "Do you have a cat?" she wondered. I said that I did not. Then she asked, "Do you at least have goldfish?" When I had said that I did not, she said that she was looking for someone with more responsibility.

Hey, I at least had a job. Besides, we could have covered this on the telephone.

> *Dakota: Filterless Camels*

Dakota lived in New Jersey and commuted everyday to her job as a computer technician for one of the large American credit card companies in downtown Manhattan. She said that she was also a part-time trainer at one of the health clubs near where she was living.

Her photos were terrific, she was in excellent shape. I am also into working out so I figured, if nothing else, we had that in common. On the telephone we talked about each of our training regimens and had decided to meet at a small lounge near her office.

Dakota was shorter than I thought, but she was very cute. She also had cute voice and terrific sense of humor. When we had initially met, I was surprised to see how she was dressed. She said that her job required her to dress down as she could get quite dirty. But, Dakota looked as though she had been working on her car. I mean, she was coming out on a date; couldn't she have, at least, washed her hands? I knew that this would not work out. We also had quite a different taste in music and movies.

On top of that, very surprisingly, I had learned that she smoked and, and of all things, they were filterless Camels.

> *Jacey: You need a Doctor*

Her name was Greek, she said, and meant "The Healer." That was very appropriate as Jacey was a Psychologist, in private practice. She was quite busy and didn't have much time for a social life, let alone afford the time to required to find Mr. Right.

I met Jacey for a drink one evening and just didn't feel a connection. There were a number of reasons but, in short, I didn't think that we had enough in common. She was extremely intelligent, spent most of her time reading psychology books and frankly, I didn't think that I would be able to keep up with her. She said that she did not agree.

One week after our date, I had gotten a call from Dr. Jacey. She said that as we were no longer dating, she would be able to see me as a patient, provide me "counseling" if I had interest. I told her thanks but thought that I needed more of a "specialist."

> *Odette: You're not helping me*

Her company had downsized and let many of the employees go. Odette had been out of work for quite some time. Ours was also a short communication.

I could hear the frustration in her voice as she told me about the many things that she was doing to find another job. She dismissed one idea after another and soon became hostile as I tried to help her.

Finally I told her that she spend more time looking for a job than trying to find a date.

> *Alma: Circus*

She could have been part of the Big Apple Circus, which happened to be in town. Alma's overcoat, hat, dress and boots where all made of animal hide-prints. I think that the coat was Zebra, the dress and boots were Cow. I didn't know what the hell that hat was, maybe Pony or Alpaca. Now listen, I'm into fashion but come on. She was fashionable sure, but not to my taste and apparently to no one else's either.

I waited for Alma at the bar of the restaurant where we would meet for drinks. It was on a Sunday afternoon, the place was packed with the Brunch crowd and very noisy. I thought the hustle and bustle would be good, no one would notice that we are on our first date. I had often gotten that "look" from other patrons when they could tell that you were meeting a woman for the first time. This time would be different.

When Alma arrived, the entire place, and I mean the entire place, came to a stand still. Except for one busboy that dropped his tray at the first sight, you could hear a pin drop. Man, it was quite a scene.

One teen age boy sitting with his parents started making the sound, "Moooo, moooo," the entire place laughed, and unfortunately, this included me. Alma left immediately. I had tried to stop her but she just kept going.

Later that evening I called Alma and told her that I felt bad [for her], she was pissed. But hey, I didn't tell her what to wear.

> *Abbie: For Sale*

Abbie was a real estate agent working in Manhattan. She specialized in high-end apartments on the West Side, downtown. I know that they have to be this way in cut throat New York, but she was what I consider to be a typical real estate salesperson, quite aggressive and I do not mean assertive. Abbie had a take-no-prisoners attitude, ready to deal [negotiate] at a moments notice. She seemed perfectly suited for the job.

She lived in chic buildings that were renovated after 9/11. I knew the building so I assumed that she was doing well, because "it ain't cheap" living down there. Abbie was divorced and had no children so she could spend all of that commission on herself. From her photos I could see that she dressed very well so I assumed that she did.

Now, I should tell you right up front that I'm not real enamored with real estate folk. I group them together on what I call my "Fatal Five List," which includes Lawyers, Doctors, Recruiters (Headhunters) and New York City Taxicab drivers. But hey, that's another book.

Her profile sounded more like an advertisement, than a bio for dating. Now, I'm not going to lie to you, when we spoke on the telephone, Abbie sounded "easy," and this was my reason for meeting her. I needed some easy and I go on record here, the idea to "wink, wink" get together was hers. I did mention that she was aggressive, right?

Abbie and I were going to meet at one of the newest lounges, called BED. Now, I'm not sure what you may be thinking, but BED was simply a warehouse size place in the Chelsea area with a clubby atmosphere and instead of couches and tables, it was filled with these luxurious beds. The emphasis was on what they called "horizontal eating and drinking," not for sleeping. I had been there before and figured it would be fun.

She was all over me and I didn't stand a chance, honest. After a few vodka tonics and a few appetizers, I was like putty in her hands. Abbie was a good looking woman and any man, and I mean *any man*, would want to sleep with her. You might say that I fell into that category as well.

Before leaving her apartment, which is where we had spent the next several hours, she handed me a folder containing brochures of her listings. She said that I now "Owed her one," and if I, or any of my friends were looking for an apartment she was to be called.

It was quite the little "sales pitch" and I told her that I would keep her services in mind.

> Iris: Are those real?

In her profile, Iris wrote that she was an "entertainer." This meant, I would learn later, a freelance belly dancer. It's a noble profession and for sure, somebody has to do it. I had been to parties in the past where they hired a belly dancer for fun and entertainment but until now, I had never dated one. In her case, it eliminated the need to visit the gym, she was in excellent shape.

At her suggestion, we met at a "Shisha Bar" where she had gotten her professional start. She said that the place had low tables where you sat on pillows and enjoy smoking flavored tobacco from as Hookah pipe while enjoying food and drink. Other than a cigar once in a while, I was not a smoker but it sounded like it would be a fun experience.

Late in the evening, the place really came alive and the several belly dancers would entertain patrons, and of course, they would drag you out onto the floor to participate. There was even a belly dance, Conga-line, and everyone, including me joined in.

As I had expected, it was a fun date and Iris was a fun companion. Born in the US to parents of Middle Eastern decent, Iris was an exotic and alluring woman with an intriguing personality. We drank, ate, [belly] danced and smoked from our personal Hookah pipe. We were having a terrific time.

At the time, I was wearing my hair a bit longer than usual. It was wintertime and I had figured the longer, the better as the warmer it would be. It was my [real] hair but I hadn't had a trim in some time and one could certainly accuse my hair of being somewhat un-kept, particularly for me. Only half-kidding, Iris had commented that it looked as though I may have been wearing a "piece." I assumed that our discussion was going to focus on appearance, but I would quickly learn that this was not acceptable. I was curious too and had a question for her as well.

Iris was, as they say, very well endowed. I asked, "Are those real?" gesturing to her chest. Iris was insulted and apparently, I would never find out.

> *Nicola: Goodfellas*

Nicola, or Nickie, as she was known to her friends was from Staten Island. She was the only girl of six children, she had five brothers. She wrote that they were all in the family business and her profile said that she was a secretary. Her father was her employer.

Nickie preferred to "chat" via email. So much so that it seemed this relationship would be nothing more than pen pals. I eventually wrote that sometime we would need to speak on the telephone, perhaps meet. She was reluctant to do so.

I thought perhaps Nickie had a heavy New York accent because often, I had found that for a variety of reasons such as language or accent, many women were reluctant to speak on the telephone.

Finally, Nickie wrote in her email that she would consider taking our communication offline but had one rule: I couldn't ask her about the family business. I never did, we never spoke.

> *Janet: Wake up!*

I had dated Janet several times and it seemed that our relationship was starting to take off. We had met for dinner a few times, ran in the Park and had even talked about taking a trip to Los Angeles where she had family. In short, we never would get that far.

Janet had invited me to the new apartment she had just purchased on the Upper East Side. I had experience in this area so I helped her navigate through the negotiations and mortgage process. She was making dinner as her way to thank me.

After dinner, Janet had asked me to stay over for the night. This was also her first night sleeping in the apartment and as you could imagine I was excited and of course I would stay. Jokingly, she said that this would be like a "test-run." I found out just how serious she was, there was an underlying reason for me to stay and it had nothing to do with sex.

Janet had two cats, although to me they were more like mini tigers. They had already staked out their claim to the place and ruled the territory like a mini jungle. If I sat in a chair that was theirs, they let me know it; scratch, hiss, bite and roar. There was no meow coming from either of these two felines. And, if looks could kill, I was already dead.

I didn't have any clothes with me so I would have to sleep in the buff. Janet on the other hand, seemed to have on more pieces of clothing than most campers. I recall at one point, she even had on a Parka but assumed that she would strip once we went to bed. She did not and I quickly realized that this was not going to be my night; I can only tell you that I had tried.

Early in the morning, we were both woken by her two cats. One was actually on top of my chest, making a noise that could only be described as growling. The other sat at the end of the bed watching me with that typical cat stare.

It was clear that her cats did not like me and Janet said that unfortunately, I did not pass the test. I was wondering, who would?

> *Mallory: Research*

You're writing a what? That was the question Mallory had asked when I mentioned that I was writing a book about online dating. Now, I didn't give her any details but realized that this was a big mistake. Hey, I was just making conversation but I haven't seen that kind of look since I was a kid and really pissed off my Mom. I knew that our date, let alone the relationship, was going to go down hill from there.

We met for drinks in the Meat Packing District. Mallory was the daughter of a former professional golfer from Long Island and said that she traveled and played with her dad often and had a four-handicap. Now, I am also a golfer and envisioned a series of golf lessons that would get me beyond my current level of play. At least in my mind, I may have been "pulling out the clubs" too soon.

I can only describe the conversation up to this point as futile. Other than the talk about golf, it seemed that we had nothing else to discuss, or in common. Talking, or rather I would say trying to get to Mallory to talk, was like pulling teeth. She didn't offer much in the way of conversation and I had quickly become bored. So, I mentioned the book.

To her credit, Mallory did know a lot about golf and I actually did get some helpful advice. But I could also see that she was stymied by the idea of my book. She continually came back to it even though I tried desperately to change the subject. I would ask, "So, how did you like traveling with your dad while he was on tour?" But she responded with, "How many people are in this book?" I continued,

"When did you finally move into Manhattan?" To which she asked, "Is this some kind of relationship book?"

I know that I brought it up, but she was asking questions that I had not been prepared to answer. Mallory had accused me of dating for the sake of research for my book. She wasn't that far off and it seemed that our date was going to be over soon. Well, "there goes the golf lessons," I had said.

As she was leaving, Mallory stopped, turned toward me and said, "Keep me the F*&% out of your book!"

Good news Mallory, you made the cut!

CHAPTER 18

Love Lost and Lessons Learned

What I've learned

I have loved two women in my life. The first, Liza, who I was married to for twenty years, and then another woman, Anda, whom I met through online dating after my divorce. I lost both of them because of my own stupidity, stubbornness, insecurity and immaturity. But, I am thankful that they had been part of my life.

I had met my future wife in high school. We were voted "Class Lovers" in our yearbook. Although we had an on again/off again relationship, we both knew that we would end up together, get married and spend our lives together. Although we had both dated other people, we got married, very young, without really experiencing the world.

We had a terrific marriage, envied by many of our friends and even families. Tough at times, but overall it was terrific having someone to come home to every night. She was my best friend, my lover and my confidant. Who could ask for more than that?

So, what happened?

I don't want to dwell on it as there are many reasons that lead to our decision to divorce. But in short, we forgot about what it was that brought us together and what made us both happy. We become very introverted and not sharing our feelings.

She was the only person that kept me going and made me feel alive. Regardless of the situation, I could tell her anything and she would always give me encouragement. But, in time, we both lost the ability to communicate with each other in the same way that kept us together for twenty years. We became roommates and lost interest in having sex.

Although there are many, the one big lesson that I'll take from this, it is that communication is a key component to any healthy relationship/marriage. Now, I'm not a therapist or counselor but I can tell you this, you can find an ideal mate, have a terrific relationship for awhile, but if you don't [continue to] communicate, you will become very, very unhappy. This is a lesson that I have learned on several occasions in both my personal and even professional life and hopefully you will learn from my experience.

My divorce became final very quickly. We had no children, wrote our own divorce agreement, and aside from that fact that the legal community can cause more problems than necessary, things went rather smoothly. I am continually asked if we are still friends, to which I respond, "We are still friendly." Perhaps some day it will be more than that but for now, I am OK with our relationship. I knew that we would both find the happiness that we lost in our marriage. At least for me, I had made it my priority.

I had recently learned that Liza had remarried and although we were divorced, I must admit that it hurt. It felt as though a piece of me had been taken away. But I also realized that she deserves the happiness that we had lost later in our marriage and I wished her well.

After a few months of hammering it out on the bar scene, often trying to be something I'm not, I read about online dating. I mean, I knew it existed, but I also thought that it had the stigma I spoke about earlier. But then, the more I found out about it, the more it convinced me that it would work for me. I decided that I would give it a try.

My first step was to find someone to take some new photos. I knew that the photos that I had of myself just weren't going to jump out of a profile. One mistake that I often see on other profiles is that the photos, well, stink. Hey, I didn't make it happen, but you know as well as I do that we live in a very superficial world and people out there are looking for someone that looks good. I cannot tell you how many individual profiles I have seen with the same photo (like a headshot), just in a different position. Come on, you don't need to spend gobs of money on a professional photographer, but at least talk a friend into taking some . . . headshots and body shots. Don't simply take photos of yourself in the mirror!

Now, I am not advocating that one should alter photos or go crazy, but I can tell you that if you put some great photos online, your chances to gain attention will increase.

And listen, if you are one of those people that think you should be noticed for who/what you are . . . . *good luck!* You may be a terrific person, but if you do not get noticed, who will ever find out?

After getting some new photos, I jumped onto the website(s) that I had decided to use and wrote copy for the written part of my profile. My profile was real and told the story of me, in brief. That's another mistake that I often see on other profiles. Some people try to write their life story online, or perhaps look at this as their creative outlet. My advice is to keep it short and sweet, I mean, if you want to write your autobiography or a great novel, write it, just not on your online dating profile. You should look at your Profile just as you would your resume when looking for a job. On your Profile, tell your story in short-form. That way, it will actually get read.

I had found that the more time I spent "working" the dating websites, the more activity I had. Again, I'm not bragging, but I was very successful. In a short period of time, I had been in contact with over 1000 women. Now listen, I'm not ashamed to admit it, but I'm not an exceptional looking guy. Just look at my photo on this book. But, I can tell you that the better your photos and the more active you are on the dating website, the more contact you will have. Don't expect that by simply posting a Profile, your social world will suddenly come together and make sense. Look at the photos, read the profiles and make contact with those that interest you. Once you have made contact, you can be selective and determine whom you would actually like to meet. I'm sure that you can take it from there.

Love Lost

I told you that online dating works, and it does. A few months after I had started doing online dating (and a short time after my divorce), I found Anda. It was almost too good to be true.

After our initial contact (I contacted her first) and a few phone conversations, the first date was at a local restaurant and we hit it off, immediately. I know that it always doesn't happen that way, sometimes it takes a lot of time and effort to get to know someone and I'm OK with that. But with us, it happened much sooner. We talked for hours about our lives, where we were from, shared stories of our jobs, friends, family, plans for the future and even about our ex's and divorce, a said no-no on a first date. I was actually interested in what she had to say and she was equally impressed with my life as well. She had a fantastic personality *and* she was gorgeous. She was from Spain and I loved her accent. We decided to see each other again and agreed that we would not tell anyone that we had met through online dating.

I mentioned that it seemed too good to be true. I couldn't get it through my thick head that in such a short period of time, I could have actually found "the one," or, at least someone that was genuinely interested in me. I kept asking myself, "How could I be this stupid" and I think that my own insecurities began to set in.

Besides my own issues, for a number of reasons, our relationship was on again/off again but during our time together, it was terrific. I had never met anyone like Anda. We traveled, locally and internationally and had a great time. We were adventurous, learned to ski, ice climb and went to the beach hired often. We both enjoyed the theater, restaurants and movies. She was equally comfortable in heels or flip-flops. And yes, the sex was absolutely fantastic. We were starting to become very, very close and I had fallen deeply in love. Anda had said that the feeling was mutual. It was perfect.

After my divorce, I had thought that I would get married again, maybe even start a family and have children (the children my first wife and I never had). Anda and I were going to make each other happy and have a terrific life together. It was going to be so cool!

Now, I am not the kind of guy who has trouble making decisions, but when it came to Anda, my life was so drastically changing that I was scared and couldn't reason. We were talking about things that I had never considered before and I was becoming unsure about what I had gotten myself involved in. I knew that I loved her deeply, but did I really want to change my life? Soon, I began to self-destruct the relationship. I blamed her for all of the things that weren't going right in my life. It was a pitiful and I was pitiful. Here was a guy that always knew what he wanted, did everything to get it and I was about to lose the best thing that had happened to me in a long time.

Loosing Anda was perhaps, the greatest tragedy in my life. I was miserable. Not only did I find the perfect woman for me (again, online), but she had also shown me the most important things in life. Things I had never learned in my many years or was afraid to admit. Anda truly made me a better man.

What I had learned from my relationship with Anda is this. Think about what you want really hard and be ready for the kind of relationship that you say you are looking for . . . because it may just happen. And, when you find it, don't screw it up, like I did. I have learned that *Love* is not always enough so do everything you can to keep it alive and interesting. Trust me, the alternative is much less enjoyable. Remember the old adage, "You never know what you have until you have lost it."

As for me, I am serious about my social life again. I may just put up a new profile and get back into it. Plus, I've got more stories to tell ya, maybe I'll write another book!

The End

www.ingramcontent.com/pod-product-compliance
Lightning Source LLC
Chambersburg PA
CBHW051256050326
40689CB00007B/1214